THE ONLINE HUSTLE

THE ULTIMATE
E-COMMERCE GUIDE

THE ONLINE HUSTLE

THE ULTIMATE E-COMMERCE GUIDE

E-Commerce: No Longer 'Why?', but 'How?'

With so many people starting e-commerce businesses, it's never been more important to get it right.

CONTENTS

INTRODUCTION

E-COMMERCE:
SOME THINGS TO CONSIDER

When historians look back on the Covid-19 pandemic, one lesson in the field of human behaviour will become readily apparent: it was the time when online shopping genuinely entrenched itself in the buying habits of people around the world.

No longer was this a 'novelty, once in a while' activity. It now became the established way in which millions of people secured everything, from medicine to clothing to food supplies.

To be fair, e-commerce had been growing steadily long before Covid-19. But with the brick and mortar retail networks closed during the lockdown, e-commerce moved to centre stage in order to fulfil basic requirements.

Consider the following: e-commerce sales have experienced a staggering increase since the start of the crisis. Not surprisingly, areas like medical supplies and household cleaning goods have seen the greatest rise, but when you consider traditionally in-store shopping categories such as food and beverage gaining recognition among customers across various age groups, you can start to discern genuine changes in core shopping habits.

Will e-commerce maintain all, or close to all, of its market positioning once the crisis has passed? While we can't tell for sure right now, the following phenomenon would suggest it will be able to keep much of its share of wallet.

- The crisis has forced many to use e-commerce for the first time. Marketers will tell you that the first step in the change of any buying habit is the most difficult. With Covid-19, that step has been taken.

- Different ages and interest groups demonstrated different attitudes towards online shopping e.g. young adults' behaviour vs. adults vs. older adults, or Gen Z vs. Millennials vs. Gen X. What is certain is that for some age groups in the face of the virus, taking a bold step into the world of e-commerce was fairly easy to make, whilst for some others there is room for improvement.

- And while shoppers might like to mix up their shopping habits between online and brick and mortar, it might become difficult if they're in a region where retailers may have shuttered some of their stores.

At the end of the day, we won't know for some time what the actual net effect of Covid-19 will be on the e-commerce world, but we do know that it will continue to grow and grow at a very significant rate.

THE BENEFITS

Covid-19 may have forced people to dip their toes into the online shopping world, but once in, the overwhelming majority have found it a comfortable place to do business.

Taking advantage of next-day delivery can become very alluring, particularly when you've sidestepped a lot of other shopping hassles such as parking and queuing. To top it all off, the ease with which goods can be returned is also a very powerful draw.

What does this mean for you?

Sometimes in life, it takes a traumatic event to bring about genuine change. If you're a brick and mortar retailer who is thinking of expanding through the internet or has already even started down the path, this guide could be invaluable. For everyone else, we would strongly recommend you look inside yourself, summon up the resolve and the commitment, keep us by your side and let's take a journey that can and should be profitable.

The world does not exist in a vacuum. We know for a fact that large numbers of retailers over the past several months have been making plans to enter the e-commerce world; some embracing a mixed model, some turning their backs entirely on a conventional store operation. It would be a mistake to believe that the strong growth trajectory of e-commerce guarantees success for anyone who jumps into the market; nothing in the business world is risk-free and you are well founded to have questions across all sorts of topics, including market research technology, legal, tax and distribution. In the coming chapters, we will be discussing in greater detail those areas mentioned above.

We'd like to close this section on a personal note. We know that what you're about to embark on is challenging. If you weren't anxious there would probably be something wrong with you. But keep this in mind: if you chew this off in bite-size pieces in the company of a competent consultant, there is no reason why you can't make it as far as you want to go.

DO YOUR MARKET RESEARCH:

THE MORE YOU KNOW, THE BETTER YOU DO

Market research is a critically important element of launching an e-commerce business. It is also an element that has a multitude of facets, each as important as the other.

Let's consider the primary questions that market research should answer:

- What problems or needs are you trying to address?

- What's the size of the market you're seeking to enter in a particular country?

- What are the purchasing habits of your potential customers?

- What are the various legal and regulatory challenges to entering a new market?

Now if we drill down, there are a whole host of follow-on questions that the savviest marketers are keen to find the answers to:

- Can you construct a customer avatar containing a myriad of information and insights around their buying habits and personal traits?

- What are the cultural differences in the markets you are seeking to enter? Think about both product differences and buying differences.

- What product market regulations have to be adhered to? We're referring to things like plugs, sizes, CE mark, perishable vs. non-perishable items, alcoholic beverages, organic products and certification, electronics, product licensing and compliance.

Beyond those issues are the concerns involving your competition, such as:

- What level of investment are you going to need to be competitive?

- Have you identified who your competitors are? Have you learnt what their strategic trajectory is and what their strengths and weaknesses are as they pertain to the inflection points with your own offering?

- Is there anything about your offering that could provide you with an asymmetrical impact in your marketing campaigns?

- Are there any cultural sensibilities that need to be taken into account in the preparation and distribution of advertising?

Keep in mind that the underlying phenomenon to market research is simple: the more you know about your potential customers and the market in which they exist, the greater chance you'll have of connecting with those customers.

BENCHMARKING

One of the most effective and insightful methods of market research is benchmarking. Put simply, this is a way to study in detail the performance metrics of a product similar to one that you're thinking of offering for sale.

The first step in the process is to select a particular product and establish the key performance metrics, such as sales, distribution, nature of advertising and geographical reach. The next step is to choose other sellers to benchmark. We would recommend looking at both the market leader in any one product category as well as a smaller but aggressive player.

At this point, the analysis begins. Look closely at how the others market their products. What are their pricing points? What does their website look like? What do customers say in their reviews? By determining what works best for a particular product in a particular market, you can start to adapt, adjust and implement best practices for your own products.

BENCHMARKING STEP BY STEP

- Select a product to benchmark.

- Identify the key performance metrics.

- Choose other sellers to benchmark.

- Review performance based on sales, number of sellers and markets.

- Assess the features of the products (photography, listing, price and offers) and the competitors' product range and identify opportunities for improvement/solution.

- Adapt, adjust and implement best practices.

- Set achievable objectives and establish execution timelines.

A GLOBAL STRATEGY NEEDS A LOCAL SENSITIVITY

Many years ago, General Motors introduced a new family car to the American market. It was a mid-sized four-door coupé that was priced in a way that made it affordable to a wide swath of the market. It was called the Nova and it sold like hotcakes.

General Motors was so pleased with the Nova's sale performance that it decided to export them to South America. Unlike the experience in North America, the sales in the southern hemisphere were sluggish, to say the least.

And then one day, a GM executive in Argentina sent a memo to headquarters explaining that Nova ('no va') in Spanish means 'no go', hardly the name you would want associated with a car. GM quickly renamed the car, and the sales picked up accordingly.

We share this story with you for a reason: cultural sensibilities are critically important when starting the journey from your home market into new territory. They affect everything: the naming of the product, the pricing, the sizing and the advertising. One of the most effective ways to ensure that you're not running afoul of those cultural sensibilities is to reach out to those who can localise your product offering across all the relevant areas — pricing, advertising, et cetera.

THINKING GLOBALLY

We should point out that building your e-commerce market internationally carries with it a whole raft of considerations that require help in the form of localisation and translation consultants. Different countries have different cultural sensibilities when it comes to advertising, pricing and paying. For example:

- The Chinese fulfil the majority of their purchases over the phone.

- Germans are not as keen to pay by debit or credit cards compared to other North European countries.

- In America, blue is the colour most used on corporate branding. In East Asia, blue is seen as a cold, evil colour.

- Americans and the British may speak the same language, but for marketing purposes they have to be considered two very distinct groups.

We think it's safe to say that every geographical market you might be thinking about entering has its own peculiarities that have to be taken into consideration. Put simply, to expand into an international market without professional assistance invites trouble.

KEEPING YOUR HEAD ABOUT YOU

Passion is a much-needed characteristic in the world of e-commerce. You have to be committed to the product you're selling and dedicated to overcoming all the challenges that stand in the way of getting that product out successfully into the marketplace.

Unbridled passion, however – passion that overrides logic and objectivity – is not a good thing. We often see people become so obsessed with making a success of their venture that they ignore some basic objectives. If you're not achieving a sustainable profit margin, which should translate into a decent return on your investment, all of the passion in the world won't necessarily turn things around. The best businesspeople learn quickly to embrace both their hearts and their minds in building their operations. Maintain that passion to build, but use your mind to calibrate whether you are going to be successful.

To do this, you have to adjust and adapt. And to do that, you need the appropriate mix of passion and cool objectivity.

THERE IS KNOWING, AND THEN THERE IS REALLY KNOWING

Someone once said that the process of really getting to know your customers is very much like peeling an onion: there's is no end to the layers you can take off, and each one can provide a great deal of meaningful insight.

It is simply not enough to know the cursory demographics or the spending capability or the preferred payment methods of your clients. The successful e-commerce marketers are those who have committed to peeling through numerous layers to discern the subtle, and not-so-subtle, buying traits of the people they're trying to attract.

For the sake of this section, let's break things into a series of logical steps:

- Everything we buy falls into one of two camps. It is either a utilitarian purchase – a pair of socks, for instance – or a discretionary purchase – a new dress, for example. Understanding which of those gaps your product fills is the first step in formulating a marketing plan that stands a good chance of connecting.

- That brings us to the demographics of your customer base. You need to know the age bracket you're targeting, their location, their expendable income and their professional and educational status. Why is all that important? Put simply, once you understand who you are trying to reach, you will then know the best way to engage their attention and their wallet. Here are just some of the ways in which you need to tailor your outreach depending on the demographics of your customer base:

- If it's a younger audience – say, 18 to 22 – you need to tailor your website and marketing material in a graphic style that they can relate to: lots of photos, infographics and short copy blocks.

- If you're after an older segment, keep the type on your website bigger and stress any sales or any coupons that might be available.

- If you're dealing with a professional audience, style the writing accordingly and make the graphics crisp and sophisticated.

All of this requires funding: appropriate amounts of funding pre-launch, launch and at regular intervals afterwards. To miscalculate the amount of investment needed is one of the biggest causes of failure among e-commerce businesses.

Every marketing action in the e-commerce world carries with it a Return on Investment (ROI) that has to be taken into consideration, particularly when it comes to future plans.

Financial considerations are not the only things that need to be taken into account when overcoming barriers to entry.

Consider the following:

> • Seasonal factors come into play with items such as clothing, recreational goods and gardening tools.
>
> • Brand-new products often present a challenge when it comes to providing the most up-to-date information.

PLAYING IT SAFE

Seven years ago, reports started emerging of people being injured by exploding mobile phone chargers that had reportedly been built in China. It is events like those that can generate long-lasting reputational damage to the manufacturers, not to mention financial liability to address any ensuing civil lawsuits.

In today's environment, virtually every good that is sold online requires some form of regulatory sign off. Some examples include:

- Electrical goods sold within the EU must carry the CE marking to show that the product has complied with the essential health and safety requirements as indicated in the applicable European Directives and Regulations.

- In order to sell food supplements in the UK, you need to be registered and all your products must be compliant with the Food Safety Act.

- Don't make the mistake of believing that because your product has regulatory approval in one jurisdiction, it will automatically obtain warrant regulatory approval elsewhere. CBD products are allowed in several parts of the US; the UK and EU governments place certain restrictions to make sure their use is in full compliance with the law provided that certain parameters are applicable.

GROWING GRADUALLY

If you remember, at the beginning of this guide we talked about tempering passion with objectivity. Well there is another balancing act that needs to be achieved if you're interested in having long-term, sustainable success. We're referring specifically to staging your expansion in such a way that you avoid finding yourself in over your head with products that aren't selling as well as they should be.

Think about the level of investment that determines whether you can jump into the market with a small number of items or just go for a full-blown expansion. It is all about staging your expansion. The first few products will reveal the level of investment that is required and how soon/fast to add/consider new items.

OTHER THINGS TO CONSIDER

- **Don't take your eyes off the competition.** Think about your competition and any asymmetric impacts. Competition can teach you lessons in terms of photography, product listing, product variety, offers, deals, as well as from a marketing point of view.

- **Asymmetric impact.** Any asymmetric impact can be summarised in the name of Covid-19 – the business should be ready to pivot. Pivoting is essential because business circumstances can vary from season to season. Remember the fidget spinners? Back in 2015 everyone was selling these fun little accessories. However, when that trend passed, businesses without an alternative plan and no pivoting capacity were stuck with excess stock and no plan for the future.

- **Stay on top of the commercial side.** Commercials (margins, product costing, et cetera) – the business aspect of the whole venture – are essential. Our advice is to, from the very formative stages of the business, liaise with a highly knowledgeable e-commerce accountant.

LAST WORDS

We hope we've convinced you that the market research mission is critical in the e-commerce world. A certain amount of this work can be conducted using available research software, but at the end of the day, certain decisions on things like culture, language and seasonal market needs, will be down to you and you alone. Rely on your entrepreneurial instincts and your intuition and the road to success will open up in front of you.

MANUFACTURING, LOGISTICS AND WAREHOUSING

Everything within the e-commerce world revolves around the product you are selling. While that might sound rather simplistic, it should serve as a clear indicator of just how important the manufacturing process is to the success of your enterprise. The minute the quality of your goods suffers, or the minute the delivery deadlines are missed, is the moment when your business will be at its most vulnerable. Therefore, it is in your best interest to expend a fair amount of energy selecting who will manufacture your product or products.

So let's take a look at some of the things you need to be thinking about:

- To find a reliable manufacturer, either in your own back yard or internationally, requires some leg work. There is no shortage of directories and trade shows – eTradeAsia, Alibaba.com, SaleHoo, et cetera – but relying solely on others to identify the best manufacturer is a mistake. If at all possible, you need to travel to a potential manufacturer's locale and see for yourself the quality of the goods produced; you need to feel comfortable on the way to establishing long-term trust, and you need to start the process by which you're going to agree pricing (more on that later).

- If you're going to spend the time and resources to make this trip, make it worthwhile. Plan to visit more than one manufacturer and spend some time getting to know your local virtual assistants (VAs), who will be a huge help in quality assurance and delivery issues.

While we are on the subject of VAs, we should emphasise that selecting the right one can be a tremendous boost for your business. Over the years sellers have said a good VA is invaluable in handling customer inquiries such as returns or negative reviews.

A good VA can allow you to:

- Ease your day-to-day responsibilities.

- Focus on the core business aspect of your venture.

- VAs can be offshore or domestically based.

Successfully negotiating prices with your suppliers is critically important to getting your business off the ground with the right operating margins. Too often, people think that negotiations of this nature are all about driving down the price as low as possible, but the truth of the matter is there's a lot more to it. Suppliers are going to be looking at just how much business they can expect from you. Chances are, you won't have an established track record, so you will have to rely on sales projections for the time being.

It probably goes without saying, but it is not a bad idea to talk to multiple suppliers and let each of them know that you're doing so. Competitive pricing is a good thing.

Keep in mind that the price of the product itself is not the only component that goes into your operating margin. The market average for a down-payment on goods is usually 30 percent. Some manufacturers require a minimum purchase order. Those that don't may agree to a lower down-payment in return for a large bulk purchase. (Please remember to request multiple samples. You'll need them for all sorts of things — marketing, imaging, quality control, et cetera.) In a similar vein, it pays to ask for a discount on invoices paid earlier than requested. Just as you can negotiate a lower down-payment on bulk orders, you can turn that concept around and agree a larger down-payment for decrease in the cost of goods.

One of the most important points we can make around the subject of negotiation is to keep in mind the overall cultural context you're in. A European supplier will take longer to get to know you and will expect any negotiations to be carried in a calm, professional manner. In China, there is a term called *Guanxi* that speaks volumes about how to successfully do business in that country. The literal definition of *Guanxi* is 'network' or 'relationship', but it springs from a deep sense of personal trust that exists between people and which allows them to do business without worrying about the trustworthiness of each other. Seek to establish that level of connectivity with your suppliers and you will benefit tremendously. It might be a big planet but it is a small world among suppliers, particularly in Asia. We say this because you don't want to become known as a problem customer. With that reputation, nothing good happens.

One of the most important decisions you will have to make is deciding whether you rely on a manufacturer within the local area in which you reside, or reach out to an international manufacturer, most likely somewhere in Asia. Let's consider the pros and cons of those scenarios.

Going local in, say, Europe or North America carries with it the benefit of eliminating burdensome overseas shipping costs. That doesn't mean there are not any shipping costs; the costs are just more manageable. (More on shipping later in this chapter.)

There are other advantages, too:

- Reduced shipping costs free up capital that can be allocated for all sorts of things such as advertising.

- A local supplier will, by its nature, be up to speed on local and regional product regulations.

- Having a supplier in your own region will also make it easier to build a relationship which tends to result in a greater personalised service.

There are some downsides to local production, of course:

- Higher cost of goods is a distinct possibility in the non-Asian markets.

- Longer production timeframes can also be experienced.

- And finally, there is often a request for higher minimum order.

So let's look at the other side of the coin. What are the pros and cons of relying on suppliers in the Asian markets?

On the positive side:

- Higher production rates within specific manufacturing areas.

- Access to established platforms that provide access to a variety of manufacturers, such as Alibaba and Taobao.

- Extended variety of packaging, colours and sizes which means deeper specialisation in multiple product categories.

On the downside:

- Quality control always becomes more challenging from a great distance.

- Quality control can also be an issue when you are dealing with high production rates and little or no personalised service.

- Overseas sourcing of products adds up in regards to shipping times and requires robust monitoring of replenishing of goods/orders against how fast the products are sold.

A CRITICAL NOTE

Contrary to what you may have heard from people in the e-commerce world, it is by no means necessary to actually travel to China or other manufacturing spots in Asia. While that may have been true in days gone by, you can rely on competent and locally savvy VAs to be your intermediaries, and to ensure uniformity of things like production colour and quality is not compromised.

LOGISTICS

We briefly mentioned in an earlier chapter the need to smartly and efficiently manage your finances. As we now delve into the interesting world of shipping, you're going to see why that is so important. Moving your goods from one point to another is not an inexpensive proposition and nor is it always easy to calculate that cost regardless of whether it's by air or container ship.

Even though using air freight can be as much as five times as expensive as going by sea, there are two occasions when it makes sense to opt for the more expensive route:

- During the launch of the business when it's imperative that you have all your products available.

- When the amount of what is being shipped is small enough – say a sample of a product – and it is unlikely to run up an inordinate bill.

We would strongly suggest spending time becoming familiar with the various rates charged by sea and air freight companies. The rule of thumb is that sea freight is always cheaper considering that it typically charges by size rather than weight and is predictably far slower. Seaboard containers typically come in 20- and 40-foot dimensions, but if your shipment takes up less than a full container it can easily be broken up into a smaller unit and stored with other such units or shipped as mixed items of other providers.

For those sellers interested in shipping goods to Europe, there are a number of things to take into consideration. First and foremost, it pays to connect with a highly specialised shipping company that offers end-to-end service, a respected customer service culture and a knowledge of local importation rules.

Looking at things more specifically, a seller to Europe should take into account the following:

- In order for a seller's goods to clear Customs it must have an EORI unique identification number, which in turn is connected to the VAT registered number of the seller's company in Europe.

- Particularly when looking at Europe, there are two main types of import costs: import duty and import VAT. Import duty is a non-refundable cost (about three to nine percent of your costs of goods), whereas import VAT could be refundable provided that the correct shipment details and the seller's EORI number are included in the clearance documents.

- Whether or not you're selling into Europe, there are three important things to keep in mind in any import transaction:

1. All shipping and taxes are to be paid prior to the shipment. If any costs are not paid, there is a high risk of goods not being cleared on time via local Customs and you may find yourself incurring temporary storage costs there. Your shipping provider should notify you in advance of exact times and payment deadlines in order to ensure that no such occurrence takes place.

2. Make every effort to use the appropriate 'Harmonised System' (HS) code in labelling your goods. It might sound straightforward, but the truth is that there are numerous goods with very similar codes. There are a variety of import duty calculators on the internet that can assist you in reviewing and validating the HS codes of your goods. It is important to remember that VAT is not chargeable on certain goods (i.e. baby products in the UK), and that processing customs clearance with a wrong HS code can incur further costs.

3. Last, but not least, we would strongly suggest that you work closely with your tax and customs advisor on the intricacies associated with reclaiming import VAT.

WAREHOUSING

We often get asked which element of an e-commerce business is the most important. From our vantage point, they're all equally as important. Just as a car couldn't run on seven cylinders, an online retail platform wouldn't last long if one of its units wasn't up to snuff.

We make this point now because while manufacturing and marketing may seem like the critical points of the business, the ability to effectively warehouse and distribute your products is also mission-critical.

With that in mind, we will discuss the pros and cons of the following four options that can be employed to warehouse your goods:

- Merchant Fulfilment

- Outsourced Fulfilment via Amazon's FBA program

- Outsourced Fulfilment via 3PL

- Drop shipping

MERCHANT FULFILMENT

As the name implies, merchant fulfilment is the approach in which the seller takes over responsibility for the storing, packaging and shipping of products directly to buyers.

Pros:

- For those starting out in this industry, there is a certain appeal to managing your own warehousing and fulfilment. It is certainly the low-cost option and it gives you full control over the process. However, as you will read below, there are other things to consider.

Cons:

- We feel there are a number of considerations that argue against merchant fulfilment but the one that we feel is paramount has to do with your own time management. Every minute that you are focused on learning the intricacies of product delivery or ensuring that the warehouse environment is appropriate is a minute not spent on marketing your product.

Our other arguments are as follows:

- There is a need for appropriate space. Your garage may look ideal for the purpose, but if there is any leakage or pest infestation, you could be in trouble.

- If your warehouse is located far away from your customer base, you are going to struggle with timely and/or guaranteed delivery. Relying on delivery services such as DHL will solve those problems but will end up taking a significant bite out of your operating margin.

- The investment in warehouse materials – everything from management software to packing and wrapping – can also take its toll on your margins.

- Getting your head and arms around shipping regulations and selecting the best freight forwarder is not a simple business. A single mistake in this area and you're going to accrue dissatisfied customers – not a smart way to grow a business.

OUTSOURCED FULFILMENT BY AMAZON (FBA)

With Fulfilment by Amazon (FBA) you are outsourcing your logistics to one of the largest fulfilment networks in the world. This approach enables you to store your products in an Amazon fulfilment centre where it will be packed and shipped directly to your customers.

Pros:

- Considering its depth of manpower and vast warehouse infrastructure, the FBA program allows for much quicker turnaround in getting your product to your customers.

- Associated management issues – i.e. leases, staff, regulations and warehouse operating systems – are eliminated.

- You can guarantee delivery times; with Amazon Prime you can have next day delivery.

- Exposure to heavily used fulfilment options for sellers.

- Optional services such as labelling, gift-wrapping and prep are available.

Cons:

- As you might expect, anytime you outsource a business process, you inherently eat into your profit margin.

- You are turning over control of how you store and how you package your product.

- If your sales stagnate, your storage costs will rise.

- The product will arrive at the customer with Amazon's box branding, not yours.

OUTSOURCED FULFILMENT/3PL

3PL or Third-Party Logistics, is the option by which a seller can store in a warehouse outside Amazon for lower storage costs, this may be more suitable for 'long term storage' due to these lower rates.

Through 3PL, you can store in their facility, fulfil orders to other marketplaces (eBay, Shopify, et cetera.) and even appoint that 3PL provider for product returns. Remember, if you have stock overseas, Amazon will send it back to your company, for which you as the seller will need to organise shipment, all of which results in high fees and unnecessary hassle.

It is always better to have a local 3PL provider (regionally or for the continent) for storage of goods, product returns or even for re-labelling product labels (in case you push a different product line and therefore need to sort out new product labels to be sent to the FBA). 3PL is more or less a warehousing, shipping and fulfilment agent for your business, ideal for warehousing excess stock but also for selling into different marketplaces. For example, there are sellers who trade on Amazon UK via their FBA but they also store goods in warehouses in Germany or even the Netherlands as they also sell goods on other marketplaces such as CDiscount in France and Otto in Germany. It is important though to keep in mind that in order to minimise the impact on your bottom line, you have to negotiate the best possible deal with 3PL firms.

Pros:

- Significant time saving difference over self-fulfilment.

- 3PL companies can assist in labelling, pick-and-pack, returns processing and product quality control.

- Storage of excess stock and organisation of replenishment orders.

- Ability to fulfil orders outside the Amazon network – your own website, eBay, Shopify, et cetera.

- Eliminate management issues ranging from staffing, lease arrangements or computerised warehouse management systems.

Cons:

- There is a possibility that the quality of product delivery may be compromised without controls in place.

- You give up control over storage and packaging. That's

not an insignificant issue. Bad packaging can result in negative reviews, which in turn can undermine your overall investment.

- As with some of the other options, stagnating sales will result in higher storage costs.

DROP SHIPPING

In this approach, the retailer does not keep goods in stock but instead transfers their customers' orders and shipment details to either the manufacturer, another retailer, or a wholesaler, who then ships the goods directly to the customer. As in a retail business, the majority of retailers make their profit on the difference between the wholesale and retail price.

Pros:

- Easy to resume trade and can easily kickstart your online venture.

- Drop shipper (most of the time the manufacturer) holds the stock and is in charge of the shipping of the product.

- No need to engage in establishing a relationship with

the supplier as the drop shipper will do so as they hold the stock.

- Large variety of goods expansion to various categories.

- Less hassle in terms of storage and fulfilment of orders.

- No need to invest in large stock levels which helps your cashflow.

Cons:

- A vast variety of goods means limited potential in building a brand – aiming at 'a store selling everything' at best.

- Limited visibility of the item to be sold.

- Low margins: high costs for paying the drop shipper in terms of storage, fulfilment, shipment and cost of item.

- Finding the right product at the right time can be a time-consuming exercise.

- Competing on price with sellers can compromise value for your storefront.

- Limited scaling options especially when dealing with multiple dropshipping sites.

- Limited control over delivery times of your orders to your customer.

- Production can be discontinued without warning.

Warehousing options to consider for your expansion:

- Deciding on the most suitable expansion strategy depends on finding a balance between three core elements: guaranteed delivery options, good/excellent condition of the delivered product and cost-effective warehousing services along with profitable operations for your online business.

- Self-managed fulfilment is for small-scale/local-level operations and testing the waters when selling negligible volumes overseas. For sellers who have a global mindset and are looking for a scalable strategy overseas, outsourced fulfilment via FBA/3PL and, carefully combined with drop shipping is the way forward.

- A popular option is to use the outsourced fulfilment via FBA for those sellers who want to 'test the waters' overseas and are looking for an arm's length overseas presence for their business.

- A combination of outsourced warehousing via 3PL supporting the FBA operations would be an ideal solution for a) sellers who hold inventory overseas and want to mitigate long-term storage costs from FBA and fully utilise the potential of expanding via other marketplaces by using the fulfilment options from a 3PL; and b) for sellers who want to maintain a warehouse presence outside Amazon overseas that can handle storage operations, (re-)labelling, product quality, product returns when required and for supporting replenishment of the FBA in case stock levels are running low.

- Drop shipping on its own could be a short-term expansion strategy overseas with limitations on branding opportunities and questionable product continuity. It is advisable to combine drop shipping with any of the two outsourced fulfilment options by combining a standard line of products with a variable product line through drop shipping. In any case, there is a small number of sellers who can scale through drop shipping, however it is essential to keep accurate records on product costings, have integrated stock management in place and have a deep understanding of profits per item. Also, they will need to keep a good record of the stock the drop shipper has available – poor delivery from the drop shipper or being short of stock can lead to lost leads and bad reviews.

VIRTUAL ASSISTANTS (VAs)

One of the characteristics of a successful business owner is what we call 'time discipline', by that we mean knowing where your time is best spent. One way to accomplish this within the e-commerce world is by hiring a VA who has the necessary core competencies that will allow you to do what you do best.

The logical starting point in that process is to articulate exactly what the VA is to be doing for you. (Start small and you can always add to their responsibilities as time goes on.)

VAs can handle a wide variety of responsibilities. Some of the more common roles they occupy are:

- Responding to customer requests and managing any negative reviews or unpleasant customer service.

- Product quality.

- Product sourcing.

- Or any other aspect of an administrative nature that can hold back the business. IMPORTANT: a VA will know exactly in which areas this will be needed; balance needs with costs.

While there are numerous websites you can use to identify individual VAs, we would recommend dealing with professional and traceable VA providers that have developed proven expertise in matching the right assistant for the required tasks.

There are two different sets of character traits that you interview for: the first we call the 'overarching characteristics'; the second are much more specific to the needs of your business.

Overarching qualifications:

- Honest

- Reliable

- Attention to detail

- Works quickly

- Resourceful

- Ability to multitask

- Good at time management

- Strong communication skills

From there, we would suggest the following action:

- Conduct several interviews with your prospective VAs.

- Know the tasks you need to outsource to the VA.

- Request samples of previous work.

- Establish whether communication tools are in place.

- Give clear tasks to the VA and request clear outcomes – complexity kills delegation.

- Establish whether they have experience in the field.

Important skills that are crucial for any good VA:

- Strong communication skills.

- Excellent customer service.

- Excellent internet skills.

- Very good English-speaking level.

- Project management tools and reporting.

- The ability to work independently.

ONE FINAL NOTE ON VAs

Your relationship with them will benefit from giving them a clearly defined task with a clearly defined deliverable.

One favourite saying we keep in our head is: 'complexity kills delegation'.

SUMMING UP

There are a myriad of details to be considered in selecting a supplier. Hence, a good solid plan with a comprehensive checklist should be on hand. Leave no detail unturned. Over the years, one area that has been problematic for sellers is ensuring that the colour of the product they've agreed upon is the colour they receive. It's that kind of detail that can be the difference between a successful relationship with your supplier, or one laced with disruption, caused by your dissatisfaction with the quality of goods or the inability of the supplier to meet deadlines.

PRODUCT COMPLIANCE/ IP/TRADEMARK

In today's global marketplace, there have to be processes in place to ensure that products meet certain benchmarks in areas ranging from safety to environmental standards to appropriate packaging. It is only when those standards have been met that the all-important steps of securing intellectual property rights and a trademark can be achieved.

With all of that in mind, what follows is a brief overview of some of the many regulations and protocols you need to be aware of as you build your business. As we have said many times before, this is an area in which it makes sense to work closely with your business advisor to see that your compliance measures are up to date and encompassing the entire geographical reach of your business.

PRODUCT COMPLIANCE

This is one of those terms that has so many different meanings across so many different products in so many geographies.

To bring products into Europe, for example, it is necessary to secure the CE *(Conformité Européenne)* marking, which indicates the product meets EU standards in terms of quality and safety of use. It is simply a statement by the manufacturer about the conformity of the goods with European standards.

The CE requirements are lengthy, but to give you a sense of their intent here are just a few of the things you have to pay attention to:

- General product safety regulations.

- Packaging and waste directives.

- Recyling agreements relating to batteries via trash cans.

- Consumer rights.

- Different requirements (toys, medical devices and certain electronics).

- Restricted items (ensure that you have double-checked that your products do not fall under restrictive categories).

Some things to keep in mind about roles and responsibilities attached to product compliance:

- The importer of record is obliged to check diligently whether the imported goods are fully compliant.

- The importer has to ensure that the documentation and certificates are in place.

- The importer is also directly responsible for product safety.

- The importer is responsible if they place a product on the market that is dangerous or does not have mandatory certification and CE marking.

- It should also be noted that the affixing of the CE marking on goods that do not require it is also punishable.

The penalties for non-compliance are severe:

- Jeopardising the whole expansion venture.

- Audit risk.

- Opportunity costs.

- Monetary losses and cash flow risks.

Once you're confident that you've met all the required quality and technical standards, it is time to secure your product's intellectual property rights. Again, an adviser will expedite and ensure the thoroughness of the process, but here is a short-hand guide to product IP:

- Draw up technical documentation.

- Ensure that your supply chain partner has used relevant national standards.

- Collect the evidence that ensures compliance with these standards.

- Ensure that procedures are in place to guarantee compliance for repeat orders.

- Keep information available for 10 years.

- Perform tests to appropriate standards.

- Use a comprehensive requirement list as a first filter during sourcing.

- Ensure the factory performs tests to correct national standards in accordance with the region you are selling or shipping to.

- Ensure the factory delivers accurate compliance evidence on time.

And now the final step is in sight – obtaining a trademark.

It is not uncommon for e-commerce businesses just starting up to de-prioritise obtaining a trademark. We can tell you from years of experience, that this is a mistake especially if selling your own design or brand. After all the effort you've put into your business so far, to then not protect it from identify theft is careless at best.

Interestingly enough, trademarks can apply to different things: the name of your product, the design of your product, a logo or a catchphrase associated with your product. Whatever you want to trademark, our advice is to do it through a specialist adviser – someone totally proficient in all the policies and procedures for trademarks on an international basis.

From our perspective, a trademark provides benefits on two planes – tangible and intangible. To reinforce our contention that it is never too early in the life of a business to secure a trademark let's take a look at those.

Tangible:

- Makes it much easier for you to take legal action against anyone who used your trademark without permission and is in breach of your trademark rights.

- Allows trading standards officers or police to bring criminal charges against counterfeiters if they use your registered trademark.

- It is your property, which means you can sell it, franchise it or let other people have a licence that allows them to use it.

Intangible:

- Exclusive Rights.

- Builds trust.

- Shows established brand qualities.

- Recognition.

- Goodwill, especially in an exit scenario.

It is essential to stress that this book offers general guidance. Every trademark registration or any legal query is best to be addressed via a trademark specialist as monetary and time losses and brand damages could be higher if you do not follow the route of professional advice.

It is for all those reasons above, we would strongly suggest obtaining a trademark as early as you possibly can.

KNOW YOUR FINANCES

This might sound strange but staying on top of your finances can be one of the most rewarding elements of an e-commerce business. Why? Because it is the only way you can understand both your business's overall performance and the numerous inputs that can be tweaked to improve that performance.

The starting point for effectively managing your finances is the preparation of a budget and product costing. Once you start trading the income or profit and loss (P&L) statement is essential.

PUT TOGETHER YOUR BUDGET

Put simply, a budget will be your business's compass: it is a way of monitoring your investment to ensure that you achieve your goals without spending more than you anticipate. When starting out an e-commerce business it will always be handy to have your projected investment plan as well as expenses listed so that you do not end up losing more money than anticipated. You will have to be very realistic when preparing one and it would be advisable that you also distinguish between 'needs' and 'wants' as part of your budget plan. In this way you will be able to track your spending progress. You can use a simple excel spreadsheet for this where you will list your current spend as you progress.

PRODUCT COSTING

For several years we ran across an e-commerce seller who was always talking about how great his business was. He would regale us with the new products he was bringing to market and the new markets he was expanding into. And then one day it turned out he had to close his business down and declare bankruptcy. How can someone be so out of touch with the fundamentals of their own business? The answer is that it can and does happen every day across the full spectrum of e-commerce retailers, and the reason behind it is quite simple.

So, let's take a look at how you arrive at the real cost of your product and what you can then do to help drive your profitability. The starting point is to take the per-unit cost of your product. You then need to add on a per unit basis, the following:

- Packing cost.

- Product inspect/QC cost.

- Import taxes.

- Freight forwarding cost.

- Listing localisation cost.

- Product fulfilment and commission costs (if using FBA).

- Advertising cost.

- Taxes/ VAT.

Once all those component pieces are added in, you will arrive at the total unit cost, which when subtracted from the actual retail cost will allow you to see what your profit margin is.

The below is a step-by-step calculation guide for your optimum product costing in conjunction with desirable profit margins:

Unit Cost	Packing Cost	Product Inspection/ QC cost	Shipping cost	Duties/ Importation costs	Freight forwarding costs	Listing localisation costs	Fulfilment Costs (if outside FBA)	Advertising Cost	Accounting/ Tax Costs	Other Cost	VAT	Total Unit Cost	Actual Retail Price	Margin per unit	Margin %
0.00	0.00	0.00	0.00	0.00	0.00	0.00	0.00	0.00	0.00	0.00	0.00	0.00	0.00	0.00	5%
0.00	0.00	0.00	0.00	0.00	0.00	0.00	0.00	0.00	0.00	0.00	0.00	0.00	0.00	0.00	10%
0.00	0.00	0.00	0.00	0.00	0.00	0.00	0.00	0.00	0.00	0.00	0.00	0.00	0.00	0.00	20%

As for targeting a profit margin, keep in mind those margins vary widely given the size of the business. Larger e-commerce businesses can generate margins as much as 15 to 20 percent; while smaller start-ups are closer to the five to ten percent margin.

But knowing what your specific costs are for each product – particularly the fixed costs – will allow you tighten your spend in one area and loosen it in another in order to maximise the return.

What we recommend is this: if you were to take on the responsibility of staying on top of all those costs it would by extension cut into your time which could be better spent selling and marketing.

What we would suggest is to work with your adviser to construct a methodology to capture those costs. Once that is finished, the next logical step is to articulate an investment plan for the near and long-term future.

PROFIT AND LOSS (P&L) STATEMENT

In its simplest terms, a P&L statement is a summary of all – and we repeat all – your revenues, costs and expenses. One of the primary benefits of being able to quickly understand the relative health of your business is to be able to decide the best way to increase your profitability by either ramping up your revenues, cutting your costs, or both.

There is a misconception that P&L statements are only necessary for larger or more established businesses. That is not the case. Accurate records sufficient for a P&L should be kept as soon as a business starts with the goal of preparing a full statement at the appropriate intervals as required locally.

Let's take a look at the various components of such a statement:

Revenue:
- This term is interchangeable with 'sales' on an income statement. It refers to all the income that comes in from normal business operations including discounts and deductions for returned merchandise.

Cost of goods sold:
- The cost of products or raw materials, including freight or shipping charges; the cost of storing products the business sells; direct labour costs for workers who produce the products and factory overhead expenses.

Gross profit:
- This is calculated by deducting the costs associated with making and selling products from total revenue.

Operating expenses:
- This term applies to those expenses incurred in the regular operation of the business. Such expenses include rent, equipment, inventory costs, marketing, payroll, insurance and funds allocated for research and development.

Operating income:
- This figure measures the amount of profit realised from a business's operations after deducting operating expenses, such as wages, depreciation and cost of goods sold.

Net profit:
- Synonymous with net income, this figure takes the gross profit (revenue minus COGS) and subtracts operating expenses and all other expenses, such as taxes and interest paid on debt.

HOW TO CALCULATE PROFIT

To find the net profit (or net loss) of your business, here are a few formulas:

- Gross profit = net sales - cost of sales

- Net operating profit = gross profit - operating expenses

- Net profit before taxes = net operating profit + other income - other expenses

- Net profit (or loss) = net profit before taxes - income taxes

- Ending inventory = beginning inventory + purchases – cost of sales

PROFIT AND LOSS REPORT
SAMPLE: ABC LLC

For the year or period: 31 December 2020

Turnover	
Amazon Sales	Xxxxx
eBay Sales	Xxxxx
Amazon Credits	Xxxxx
Amazon Reimbursements	Xxxxx
Discounts Allowed	Xxxxx
Interest Received	Xxxxx
Total Turnover	0.00
Cost of Sales	
Import Duty	Xxxx
Amazon FBA Fees	Xxxx
Amazon Selling Fees	Xxxx
Amazon Subscription Fee	Xxxx
Carriage & Import Costs	Xxxx
Cost of Goods Sold	Xxxx
FBA Inventory	Xxxx
Reimbursements	
Miscellaneous Purchases	Xxxx
Other Amazon Fees	Xxxx

Packaging	Xxxx
Review Costs	Xxxx
Samples	Xxxx
Storage fees – 3PL	Xxxx
Transport Insurance	Xxxx
Total Cost of Sales	0.00
Gross Profit	**0.00**

Administrative Costs	
Accountancy Fees	Xxxx
Advertising – Amazon	Xxxx
Advertising – AMS	Xxxx
Advertising – Facebook	Xxxx
Advertising inc videos	Xxxx
AMEX Fees	Xxxx
Bank Charges	Xxxx
Bank Interest Paid	Xxxx
Bank Revaluations	Xxxx
Computers & Software	Xxxx
Consultancy Fees	Xxxx
Directors Salaries	Xxxx
Employer's NI	Xxxx
Insurance	Xxxx
Legal Fees	Xxxx
Miscellaneous Vehicle Expenses	Xxxx
Mobile Expenses	Xxxx
Office Stationery & Other Expenses	Xxxx

Overseas Hotels	Xxxx
PayPal Fees	Xxxx
Pension Costs	Xxxx
Pinterest Ads	Xxxx
Postage & Carriage	Xxxx
Premises Expenses	Xxxx
Professional Fees	Xxxx
Realised Currency Gains	Xxxx
Remote Workers – VAs	Xxxx
Staff Salaries	Xxxx
Subscriptions	Xxxx
Subsistence	Xxxx
Telephone & Internet	Xxxx
Training and Events Costs	Xxxx
Travelling	Xxxx
Unrealised Currency Gains	Xxxx
Virtual Office / Assistant	Xxxx
World First Fees	Xxxx
Total Administrative Costs	0.00
Operating Profit	**0.00**
Profit on Ordinary Activities Before Taxation	**0.00**
Profit after Taxation	**0.00**

A P&L starts with a header which contains the name of your business and the accounting period.

This is followed by:

- Income

- Expenses

- Net profit

ADVERTISING COST OF SALE (ACOS)

Before we move off the subject of finances, there are two important areas that need to be touched on. First, having a handle on your costs will allow you to calculate your Advertising Cost of Sale (ACoS), which is a measure of the efficiency of your advertising campaign. It is the ratio of ad spend to ad revenue (in percent). You can calculate ACoS using this formula:

ACoS = Ad Spend ÷ Ad Revenue * 100

In short, ACoS defines the level of investment for every dollar that was earned with advertising on the ad campaign. For example, let's assume that a campaign has generated $150 of advertising sales. The ads during this campaign cost $50. ACoS = 50 / 150 * 100 = 33.3%. i.e. for every dollar made, 33.3 cents have been spent.

REINVESTMENT

Our last topic in finances is one that we feel strongly about and we suggest you should too. It would be awfully nice to believe that as soon as you start your business it will begin generating enough profit for you to stash that cash in your pocket and do with it whatever you wish. Alas, that is not the real world.

Businesses succeed by sufficient re-investment – investment is necessary in order to re-order stock, build country-specific websites, buy advertising and expand into new product categories and geographies. That reinvestment may take two years; it may take five years. However long it takes, it will be worth it. Trust us.

THE TAXMAN COMETH

Of all the bits of advice in this guide, there is one piece that we think stands out among the rest: stay on top of your taxes.

Why?

There are two principle reasons. First, taxes represent a major portion of your product costings, keeping them current and in good order will allow you to understand fully what your profit margins are. Secondly, any falling behind with taxes carries with it the possibility of your business being closed, with the net result of your investment being lost.

So, with all that in mind, what follows is a quick primer on just some of the tax protocols you will be dealing with as you expand your business.

For example, let's review how VAT works in the EU. While it might sound counter-intuitive, VAT regulations in the EU are determined at a country – not EU – level. (Just one more reason to work closely with your tax and VAT adviser.)

In order to assess whether you need to register for VAT on your sales, you need to determine the following:

- Whether stock is held in that country.

- The types of supplies that are made.

- Annual level of sales turnover.

- Annual level of acquisitions of goods from other EU member states.

It might make sense to think of VAT as a two-sided phenomenon. On one side of the equation is the Input VAT that has already been paid on the goods that you are buying. The Output VAT is what you're expected to charge the customer. The difference between the Input and the Output is what should be remitted to the respective tax authorities.

The EU specifies a minimum of 15 percent as a standard rate. However, for certain items, the EU permits a reduced rate as low as five percent. For some, a zero rate is possible, and certain types of transactions, such as financial transactions, may be exempt from VAT.

One of the most difficult things to determine in a VAT calculation is in which country the transaction is taxable, and therefore the rate that should be applied. Rules for place of supply vary, particularly when considering supplies to businesses versus private individuals. It is the responsibility of the supplier to collect VAT on its sales from the customer and pay the VAT amount to the tax office. However, on occasion, the liability is passed to the customer to pay the VAT to the tax office under the reverse charge mechanism.

- Invoicing: It is imperative that invoices are raised correctly as the invoice is the document that allows deduction of input VAT. If the invoice is incorrect, a tax authority can refuse repayment of the amount of VAT paid on the associated purchase.

- Tax Point: You must understand when VAT on a transaction became chargeable and due to the tax authorities. This could be the date that the supply of goods and services was completed (general rule) but could also be the invoice date or the date the payment on account was made.

It is one thing if the journey that your product follows stays within country borders; however, there are even more VAT considerations when your customer is a private individual (B2C) and is on the other side of a border, even if it is still within the EU. If you are in the EU and your customer is a private individual in another EU country, a sale of goods is considered a distance sale. You are registered for VAT in your home country, but you must also keep track of your distance sales. This is because once they exceed a certain amount, known as a distance selling threshold, you will need to register for and charge VAT in the country to which the goods are shipped to, and stop charging VAT in the country from which the goods are shipped from.

For example, let us say you are in the EU and a growing number of your distance sales are heading across the border to Germany. If those sales total less than the German threshold of €100,000 per calendar year, you charge VAT in the country that the goods were shipped from. For any sales beyond that threshold, though, you will have to charge VAT in Germany.

Brexit and the post-2021 EU-UK rules and EU One Stop Shop rules will bring great changes in the VAT landscape (see section later, titled 'An ever-changing European (VAT) landscape').

The B2B situation for intra-EU sales is a bit different. For intra-community supplies (sometimes called intra-community dispatches or EC supplies), you will not have to charge any VAT when selling or moving goods from one EU country to another when both businesses are VAT registered with valid VAT numbers.

In Europe, Australia, and the Middle East, VAT is incorporated in the price and the seller is required to remit the collected VAT element – effectively the seller becomes a 'mini tax collector' on behalf of the government which they are trading under.

Some other things to keep in mind when considering VAT and taxes are as follows:

- **When to register:**
  From the moment you intend to send goods to be stored or to be sold in a country, it is necessary to review the requirements of registration. In most cases, you will be able to sell as an overseas seller without having to establish a company. Avoiding establishing a company is the most cost-effective solution after all, because you will not need to maintain accounting and bookkeeping functions overseas simply because VAT filings will be your sole responsibility.

- **Always keep your accountant in the loop,** especially for your overseas operations, so that there is an alignment with the overseas VAT advisor in terms of overseas activities and recording of income and tax-efficient strategies (i.e. corporate tax) for the Corp. Your company accountant should be involved in the process of reconciliation regarding income from international sources and understanding how to produce tax-efficient solutions for the business.

- **Import taxes:**
  When sending goods overseas, the seller may be required to pay import taxes for the purposes of customs clearance (i.e. import duties/import taxes). Some of them may be reclaimable and some others not. Liaise with your local VAT/sales tax advisor and your shipping provider for better clarity, especially in the pre- and post-Brexit period. Also, consider which EU country could better accommodate your customs clearance requirements, or whether it is more convenient to ship to

the UK and use a freight forwarder to Europe, especially for those trading under the PAN-EU FBA programme. There are also online import duty calculators that could give a clear understanding of possible fees.

- **Important note:**
  Import taxes have nothing to do with sales tax/VAT. Import taxes are payable before customs clearance. VAT/sales tax is payable upon sale of goods where they are stored in the country of storage. For import taxes, the shipping agent and the VAT advisor could advise. For VAT/sales tax, the tax advisor would be best to assist.

- **Different VAT schemes and options**:
  Certain countries have reduced VAT/sales tax rates on certain items (i.e. the UK is zero-rated (no requirement to charge VAT) on books, coffee, bicycle helmets, or schemes that can be beneficial (i.e. in the UK, standard rate vs. flat rate; in Europe, opting for tax on arrival).

- **Consider the Amazon Pan-European FBA programme:**
  Since 2016, Amazon have launched the Pan-European FBA programme. The programme enables e-commerce sellers to reach more customers faster and with Prime eligibility in five marketplaces (UK, Germany, France, Spain and Italy). Amazon has more than 25 fulfilment centres distributed across seven European countries (UK, Germany, France, Spain, Italy, Poland and the Czech Republic). With the Pan-European programme, sellers can ship their inventory to any of the fulfilment centres where Amazon will distribute their stock throughout their fulfilment centres in Europe based on anticipated demand. The fluidity of your stock should lead to faster shipping times and lower delivery costs. The VAT obligation through this option is that sellers

will require VAT numbers in the seven countries whereby the place of supply will take place from all the respective countries. Declarations of VAT based on the arrival or destination country could offer opportunities for VAT savings. Post-Brexit, the UK will be operating as a separate country with the remaining four main marketplaces plus the two fulfilment countries as part of the programme. Finally, intra-European movement of goods needs to be disclosed through Intrastat reporting obligations. It would be best if you consult with your EU tax advisor on the above and find out if there are any promotions on this matter.

- **Do you need fiscal representation?**
  Some countries in Europe, such as France, Spain and Italy, will require fiscal representation, for example. Also, when shipping goods to, for example, Germany without being registered for VAT, your goods will remain at Customs if tax representation is not established for the goods to be cleared.

- **Understanding that the basic compliance process VAT/ GST/sales tax differ from country to country:**
  Monthly and quarterly would be the most common timeframes.
  Tip: always keep VAT related income aside from your main account so that it does not affect your cash flow.

- **Exploring the country-specific regulations:**
  The use of a specialist agent would facilitate this process. **Outsource and maintain peace of mind, but have arm's length knowledge on the regulations and needs.**

- **Generating compliant invoice:**
  In several cases when expanding overseas you will be required to issue invoices according to local regulations and rules (i.e. in Europe, Reverse Charge VAT in B2B transactions)

- **How automated is VAT remittance?**
  In the US it is almost automated, as several online marketplaces can organise the remittance of sales tax to the respective TAs; in Europe it is strongly advisable that a tax advisor is engaged as there is still red tape in VAT filings apart from the need of having hands-on advisors such as on best VAT efficient practices, Brexit and ongoing VAT rules (in some countries VAT declarations are processed on hard copies)

- **Facing the consequences of non-compliance – tax audits:**
  Several European tax authorities are tackling VAT evasion in the e-commerce sector, where online marketplaces are to be held liable for non-compliant VAT seller accounts. Such accounts may be suspended since the liability will fall on the online marketplaces. Tax authorities will issue penalties and place surcharges if case filings are not in place or payments do not reach the tax authorities on time and within the respective deadline dates. Compliance audits may even lead to temporary account suspension on your online marketplace and put in jeopardy your whole investment which could be tens of thousands of dollars. Always stay compliant! There is more at stake when non-compliance is the case.

- **Incorporating an entity overseas vs registering for a VAT/sales tax number:**
This option is different to registering for a VAT/ GST number. Several sellers receive contradictory information from blogs, 'expert' groups and other sources. Opening a company overseas is not always necessary and is highly dependent on a few factors: regulation of the country where you want to send goods, your company's overseas expansion strategy and costs and risk mitigation. In general, opening a company overseas is in the majority of cases only recommended for sellers with hundreds of product lines, aiming to establish their own 3PL warehouse and on-the-ground presence with their staffing in a specific country.

  Incorporating a company means new business operations overseas with their own budget, (probably) staff, rental costs for a warehouse, accounting fees, capital investment and all other costs that relate to a start-up. In some cases, certain costs can be mitigated (especially if a company is not going to invest into renting a warehousing space) but overall procedures, time, investment and involvement are essentials, therefore planning prior and receiving the correct advice are critical.

  Overall, registering for VAT is more time efficient and more cost effective as there are no further obligations than remitting the VAT/sales tax obligation to the respective tax authorities. Instead, incorporating an entity could incur higher set-up costs and capital investment, requiring annual accounts filing, tax planning and general management of operations.

AN EVER-CHANGING EUROPEAN (VAT) LANDSCAPE

The UK and the EU are working towards a trade agreement to be finalised by the end of December 2020 that will govern the UK-EU relations in the post-Brexit era. Until then, the UK is still bound by the same rules of the EU single market. Whether the UK finalises a deal with the EU or not, sellers will need to establish a VAT presence in mainland Europe so that they can enjoy free trade to the mainland of Europe. Whether there will be import tariffs or not for movement of goods across the Channel or WTO rules and UK Global Tariffs remains to be seen, yet it would be advisable that sellers should have enough stock to cover demand both in the UK and Europe in the event of potential disruptions. Stock forecasting and sales planning have never been more timely.

Furthermore, staying on top of the European VAT legislation and ensuring your business is compliant with the upcoming new EU One Stop Shop rules is advised. Changes in recording transfers of goods among different European countries and a single VAT prospect from 2021 are key milestones for VAT harmonisation in Europe. Even though joint and several liability rules will apply, advanced responsibility in VAT handling falls to online marketplaces, sellers are still required to be compliant with their VAT obligations, be mindful of their import processes especially for small consignments and hold EORI numbers wherever required, to name but a few. Expert advice on these matters from an EU VAT specialist is essential in maintaining your European seller account as fully compliant and low risk.

On a positive note, Europe has a lot to offer for those sellers who can remain compliant and insist on quality products. European customers have a 'race to the top' buying mentality which differs from customers from other countries. Quality and long-term utility of a product have a priority in the European customers behaviour. In light of this, VAT rules are here to offer a level playing field among different players in different countries, and to promote fair and even competition at all levels. So may the best win!

ONE FINAL BUT IMPORTANT NOTE

Up to now we've talked almost exclusively about VAT. We would be remiss however, if we didn't mention that VAT isn't the only tax you may end up dealing with. Japan has a consumption tax for instance, and to make matters even more interesting each of the 50 US states has its own sales tax and its own methodology for recovering that tax. Different countries take different approaches to VAT. Australia has a threshold of AUD 70,000 before VAT kicks in. In places like the UAE and the EU, VAT applies from day one of operation. And finally, to reach the vast Indian market one needs to incorporate a company.

We know how confusing and daunting that must look to someone thinking about expanding their business globally. Trying to get your head around all the various rules and regulations may seem like it requires a superhuman effort. But there is good news on that front. A competent tax advisor can take the mystery and the hard work out of complying with all those requirements. There is no reason to re-think a global expansion because of tax and VAT regulations. Give that job to your advisor and continue focusing on growing your business.

ADVERTISING AND MARKETING

While we consider all the component pieces of an e-commerce business to be important, it is the advertising and marketing elements that are at the heart of your business and will ultimately determine its success.

It should also be noted that advertising in the e-commerce realm is a discipline with many different parts, all of which have to fit neatly together in order to be effective.

A logical jumping-off point to understand this world is to take a look at a Pay Per Click (PPC) strategy. When PPC first appeared on social media platforms in 2002 it revolutionised the world of advertising. Rather than cast their advertising message across a vast spectrum of publications, never actually knowing its effectiveness, an advertiser could now pay a fee each time one of their ads was clicked on in a particular social media site.

The economics of PPC were easy to understand and made sense for both the advertiser and the platform. As long as the amount in sales exceeded the cost per click, PPC made a lot of sense for an e-commerce seller, particularly those operating in a large marketplace and needing to stand out among the competitors.

The most popular types of PPC advertising are Facebook ads, Bing ads and Google ad words. When compared to the traditional methods, a PPC strategy can grow visibility for your products through search engines. Moreover, it allows you to better target your customer audience and focus on their needs. You can decide based on demographics, behaviour, ideas and geographic targeting options.

VARIABLES THAT AFFECT DECISION MAKING ON PRODUCTS

- Urgency in need satisfaction.

- Financial status and financial constraints.

- Personality traits.

- Social settings.

- Social capital.

- Culture or patterns of behaviour.

PPC strategies could build great traffic to your storefront and build recognition to the overall brand. Several PPC expert firms claim that the targeted nature of PPC-generated leads has an impact of 50 percent more compared to organic traffic. It is a speedy option to reach out to your potential customers and building IP for your storefront whilst marking your area when it comes to competitors. Effectively, PPC is a marketing boost for your investment.

An obvious downside is that for start-ups it is almost necessary yet rather costly at the same time. An expert in the field could be the right choice as such a move will save you time, allow you to focus on the business and remove the stress for any ongoing campaigns. For more experienced sellers, it is key to mention that a false selection of keywords could divert traffic to competitors whcih could harm the overall motif of the campaign.

In light of the above, we would suggest certain tips to create an effective PPC strategy:

SPECIFY THE ULTIMATE OBJECTIVE OF YOUR CAMPAIGN

- Every PPC campaign has a specific end goal to achieve which can range from brand awareness and need satisfaction, to customer loyalty. Whichever is the ultimate objective, each campaign is to be treated differently and not in a 'one-size-fits-all' mindset.

KEYWORD OPTIMISATION

- Selecting the relevant keywords goes hand in hand with the ultimate objective of your campaign. Keyword research is an ongoing exercise that is inexorably bound up with your customer avatars (see more on this topic later in this Chapter) and their immediate needs in the specific point in time when launching the campaign. At the same, keyword cannibalisation of a campaign can have counterproductive results – it is the balance and right mix that matters!

DELIVERING YOUR CAMPAIGN

- As more and more customers use multiple devices, sites and means of communicating with their brands, your options should remain open at all times. Be mindful of your spending capacity and establish daily targets by keeping in mind your product costing strategy. Always review, test, assess and pivot on the outcomes of each campaign – high conversions are key to success.

OTHER ASPECTS TO CONSIDER:

- **Localisation of listings and language:** it is essential that listings need to be localised in the respective language of each country. Even though English is widely spoken and understood across Europe and the rest of the world, listing your products in the local languages, such as German, French, Spanish and Italian, could drive more traffic to your storefront. We address below certain typical errors that are to be avoided at all costs – doing so will save time, effort and misallocated financial and time investment. Initially, classic errors occur in relation to the use of British and American English, but similar examples are to be taken into account across different languages. An expert in language and listings localisation would be essential in this process to help identify and rectify any such discrepancies.

British English		American English		British English		American English
Trousers	→	Pants		Nappy	→	Diaper
Pants / Knickers	→	Underwear / Panties		Polo Neck	→	Turtleneck
Jumper / Pullover	→	Sweater		Dressing Gown	→	Bath Robe
Pinafore Dress	→	Jumper		Swimming Costume	→	Bathing Suit
Vest	→	Undershirt		Dungarees	→	Overalls
Waistcoat	→	Vest		Bootlace/Shoelace	→	Shoestring
Wellington Boots	→	Galoshes		Bowler/Hard Hat	→	Derby
Mac (Macintosh)	→	Raincoat		Torch	→	Flashlight
Plimsolls	→	Gym Shoes		Plaster	→	Band-aid
Trainers	→	Sneakers		Sweets	→	Candy
Braces	→	Suspenders		Colour	→	Color
Suspenders	→	Hold-up stockings		Jewellery	→	Jewelry
Dressing Gown	→	Robe				

Apart from the above, there are broader elements in language localisation that need to be taken into account. These include societal codes and values, geographical locales, regional language specificity or even language code in certain age groups. Just a few misplaced or mistranslated words can turn the product listings or advertising from compelling to unintentionally hilarious, which can undermine the trust of potential customers. Be it cheap or expensive goods, linguistic barriers should be the very last element to impede any seller to launch their goods successfully into a new market, especially in Europe with a wealth and multitude of various languages.

KEYWORD RESEARCH

In its simplest form, keyword research entails the identification of all the various word combinations that could be used by a prospective buyer. But in reality, it is far more complicated than that.

A keyword strategy takes into account every decision you take based upon your findings in your keyword research project, whether it's about the content you're planning to write or how you are going to track the results.

You should begin defining your strategy by looking inward, at yourself and your business, in order to answer such questions as: why did you start the business? What are your goals? What impression do you want to make when people visit your site? It also pays to visit your competitors' sites in order to see what style of branding they're using and what keywords they're using.

Failure to do keyword research in the local language is one of the biggest reasons why sellers struggle when moving to Amazon's non-English speaking marketplaces. Keyword research should be done prior to localisation, because the top keywords identified should be prioritised when localising your sales copy. It is highly advisable to have a professional translator process the keyword research. A native's comprehensive vocabulary could unlock the potential of the goods by identifying the most suitable keywords for product listing in the local language. Irrelevant keywords will result in non-related traffic to your storefront, which will divert potential trustworthy buyers away from your storefront.

Finally, European languages have a rich vocabulary which are country-specific when describing products. Direct translation of a keyword from English into another language can produce a phrase that has a totally different meaning than intended.

CUSTOMER AVATARS

The better you know your customer, the greater the chance of turning a click into a sale. You will hear the word avatar used in this context; it simply refers to a representation of your ideal customer in a way that allows you to understand their habits, their tendencies, their shopping patterns and so forth. It is by keeping track of these sensibilities that you can improve the chances of staying connected to your client base.

We hope you noticed we used the words 'ideal customer' as opposed to 'average customer' - that's an important distinction. E-commerce businesses that seek to engage with an average customer can find themselves with a marketing strategy that is too broad to be profitable. By building a model of an ideal client who has the ability and inclination to be a repeat customer, you will be much better situated.

What goes into an avatar? If you can answer the following questions about your ideal customer, you are on your way to building a quality avatar:

- Age, sex and marital status.

- Income and profession.

- Lifestyle.

- Aspirations.

With a strong avatar in hand, you can now create more targeted advertising and provide an improved user experience that facilitates repeat business.

WEBSITES

You don't necessarily have to build a country-specific, local language website in the areas that you seek to expand, but we would strongly recommend doing so for the simple reason that it allows you to show a cultural sensitivity to your client base. It also makes sense if you augment that website with a presence on all the relevant social media channels – Facebook, Instagram, et cetera.

However, in order to achieve that benefit, you have to demonstrate that you truly understand the cultural sensibilities of the country in which you're operating. To begin with, using a competent translator will allow you to take into account all the differences in language as highlighted in the previous section.

Beyond the language though there are other characteristics of a website that speak to the cultural sensibilities of a country, such as the colour palette, the size and character of the type and the overall feel of the site. A good translator will be able to lead you to the right place in this regard.

One final point: savvy customers have always been sensitive to buying habits driven by key days and events at different times of the year. The major holidays are the obvious ones, but being aware of school holidays in different countries for instance can be very helpful if you're selling products that are necessary for a holiday. Similarly, Mother's Day and Father's Day carry their own moments of marketing potential; also not to mention Black Friday, Cyber Monday, Halloween, Bank Holidays or National Holidays and other key celebration days across the world.

To sum up, don't be fooled into believing that a PPC advertising strategy is easy. It's about a lot more than feeding the social media platforms as a way to steer clients your way. It requires constant care and attention to find the most appropriate key words and the most culturally engaging web and social media sites.

Like many aspects of e-commerce, it pays to understand what's going on, but it also pays to have some dedicated help to make sure you get it right.

GOING GLOBAL

Once you've established your business, with all the focus that requires – both on your product offering and the inherent administrative requirements – it is time to think about expanding outside your home borders.

Indicative list of marketplaces in Europe per selected sector

Books/Music/Movies and Other

UK	DE	FR
Bonanza	OTTO	Fnac
Ccoolshop	Rakuten	Cdiscount
Etsy	Etsy	DARTY
Fruugo	Fruugo	Auchan
GAME	Real	Intermarche
OnBuy.com	Joom	Vidaxl
TOPHATTER		

ES	IT
Fnac	Ibs.it
Carrefour	Eprice
Casa del libro	Fruugo
Worten	Vidaxl
Etsy	Joom
Vjoom	

Clothing/accessories and Other

UK	DE	FR
ASOS	Yatego	Auchan
Zalando	Wish	Bonanza
Spartoo	Rakuten	ASOS
Wish	ASOS	Brandalley
Secret Sales	Spartoo	Etsy
Onbuy.com	Real	Venca
Vidaxl	Fruugo	Rue du
Harvey	Joom	commerce
Nichols		

ES	IT
Spartoo	Saprtoo
Zalando	Eprice
ASOS	Zalando
Carrefour	ASOS
Bonanza	Etsy
Etsy	Joom

Electronic Devices and Other

UK	DE	FR
Bonanza	Yatego	Fnac
Ccoolshop	Manomano	Cdiscount
GAME	Back<market	DARTY
Joom	OTTO	BUT
Mano mano	Real	Auchan
Onbuy.com		Back<market
Tophatter		Pixmania.com
		Rakuten

ES	IT
Back<market	Ibs.it
Fnac	eprice
Bonanza	fruugo
Privalia	vidaxl
Worten	Joom

Indicative list of marketplaces in Europe per selected sector

Pet products and Other

UK	DE	FR
Bonanza	fruugo	fnac
Joom	bonanza	Cdiscount
Fruugo	joom	le bhv/marais
Onbuy.com	OTTO	Auchan
Tophatter	real	fruugo
Vidaxl	yatego	pixmania.com
	rakuten	Rakuten

ES	IT
Fnac	Fruugo
Bonanza	Vidaxl
Privalia	Joom
Tiendanimal	Tiendanimal
Carrefour	
Worten	
Vidaxl	

Furnitures, Interior & Other

UK	DE	FR
Bonanza	Fruugo	La Redoute
Joom	Bonanza	Conforama
Fruugo	Joom	Houzz
Onbuy.com	OTTO	Galeries Lafayette
Tophatter	Wayfair	Fnax
Vidaxl	Yatego	BUT
Wayfair	Rakuten	Camif.fr
		Dela aison
		BRANDALLEY
		Metro
		VENCA

ES	IT
Fnac	Fruugo
Bonanza	Vidaxl
Privalia	Joom
Carrefour	Eprice
Worten	
Joom	
Etsy	

In addition to those mentioned, Europe and the US also share almost the same numbers of sellers trading under their marketplaces by showcasing Amazon. The average e-buyer clicks on almost nine pages on US marketplaces, whereas 8.2 times on EU sites. Overall, traffic on US sites is higher by 33 percent compared to the EU sites (based on number of clicks) with Amazon.com being the most clicked site in both the US and Europe, whilst Amazon.co.uk leading click traffic in Europe.

The challenge to that expansion is picking the right marketplace to sell in in order to reach the appropriate client base, and be comfortable that both logistics and administration are in good hands.

So, the question then becomes: how do you ensure that your marketplace selection is the correct one?

Well, the good news is that there are some helpful websites that will give you a very thorough look at all the different marketplaces operating within a multitude of different countries.

The one that we would recommend is:

https://www.great.gov.uk/selling-online-overseas/markets/results/?page=1

But identifying the various marketplaces is just the first step. What needs to happen next is consideration of the following parameters:

- **Fulfilment/Logistics:** Let's take a look at Amazon, which is a leader in this sector where it operates in currently 16 marketplaces worldwide. Its Amazon FBA also offers you easy launch, limited timetables, convenience and global reach. On top of all that is Amazon's ability to deliver goods securely and from warehouses in decent proximity to the seller.

THE 16 AMAZON ONLINE STORES WORLDWIDE IN 2020			
EUROPE	ASIA-PACIFIC	MIDDLE EAST	AMERICAS
United Kingdom	Japan	United Arab Emirates	United States
Germany	India	Turkey	Canada
France	Australia		Mexico
Spain	Singapore		Brazil
Italy			
Netherlands			

But if you were to use a smaller marketplace you would undoubtedly need a 3PL in order to minimise costs, manage stock and explore the potential in different seller-fulfilled (or not) marketplaces, even when selling via their own website.

- **Client demographics:** While the larger marketplaces have a wide-scale offering of products, it is worth identifying those speciality markets that deal in particular items such as women's shoes or sporting goods. There is no reason you can't be in more than one marketplace, but only if the expenses do not take a toll on your bottom line.

- **Competition:** This may seem obvious, but your competitors have landed on various marketplaces for a variety of reasons. It pays to understand what their motivations have been. If you find they are able to attract a particular type of customers at a cost that is favourable to them, then you might want to consider joining that marketplace.

- **Cost/benefit analysis:** At the end of the day, operating with a profit margin that makes sense for you is what e-commerce is all about. In picking marketplaces abroad, you must consider all the various costs associated with a foreign launch – platform fees, logistic costs, customs and taxes.

CULTURAL CONSIDERATIONS

It is easy to believe that the widespread fluency of the English language naturally leads to one common, global language. But we all know that is not the case. Just looking at the English language, both spoken and written in the United States and the United Kingdom, you can see countless examples of different definitions emanating from the same word. The wrong usage for some of them can easily result in a embarassing situation.

The takeaway is that it's important to secure the services of a translator in any foreign expansion; someone who can not only help you through the difference in definitions but also ensure that your marketing face off, including website, are put together in a way that resonates with local cultural sensibilities.

Last but not least, you should open a currency account. When trading in different currencies you may incur additional costs through international fluctuating exchange rates. Savings from transactions across different currencies could be a significant portion of your next purchase of goods for your next shipment.

Now that you have already been trading in your home country and are looking for other marketplaces available on the global stage, we can provide you with a checklist on aspects to consider before expanding (or whilst trading) overseas:

How to achieve global success
9 TIPS ON HOW TO EXPAND YOUR BUSINESS GLOBALLY

1. Have you done thorough research for your potential products?

2. Have you studied your competitors and calculated your price premium?

3. Are you confident with sourcing and packaging services?

4. Are you familiar with shipping your goods overseas to new marketplaces?

5. Are you well-versed with international VAT rules and procedures?

6. Do you sell products that require linguistic localisations?

7. Are you able to calculate the frequency of replenishing your existing stock?

8. Are you capable of managing your own income and expenses?

9. Have you explored other opportunities and diversified your income investments?

WRAPPING UP

We thought that, if we summed up each of this guide's sections, it would give you a good at-a-glance sense of what it takes to succeed in the world of e-commerce – so let's go.

MARKET RESEARCH

It pays to look at this from both a macro and a micro perspective. On one hand it's important to understand the entire marketplace you're seeking to do business in. On the other hand, you need to build a client avatar in order to fully appreciate all the habits and sensibilities of your ideal client.

One of the most effective and insightful methods of market research is benchmarking; put simply, benchmarking is a way to study in detail the performance metrics of a product similar to one that you're considering selling.

One element of market research deals with how your product can reach across any cultural gaps that may exist – whether it be with the product's name, colour or any other element that requires translation from the home market to a specific international market. It is simply not enough to know the cursory demographics, the spending capability or the preferred payment methods of your clients.

The successful e-commerce marketers are those who have committed to peeling back numerous layers to discern the subtle and not-so-subtle buying traits of the people they're trying to attract.

BARRIERS TO ENTRY

Too many people these days equate building an e-commerce website with building an e-commerce business. But nothing could be further from the truth.

One might be a component piece of the other, but a sustainable business requires repeat customers who can rely on secure payment systems and speedy delivery of goods.

GROWING GRADUALLY

Think about the level of investment which determines whether you can jump into the market with a small number of items or just go for a full-blown expansion? It is all about staging your expansion. The first few products will reveal the level of investment that is required and how soon/fast to add/consider new items.

GUANXI

In China, there is a term called *Guanxi* that speaks volumes about how to successfully do business in that country. The literal definition of *Guanxi* is 'network' or 'relationship'. But it springs from a deep sense of personal trust that exists between people that allows them to do business with each other without worrying about the trustworthiness of each other. Seek to establish that level of connectivity with your suppliers and you will benefit tremendously.

PLAYING IT SAFE

In today's environment, virtually every good that is sold online requires some form of regulatory sign off. Don't make the mistake of believing that because your product has regulatory approval in one jurisdiction, it will automatically warrant regulatory approval elsewhere.

MANUFACTURING, LOGISTICS AND WAREHOUSING

The minute the quality of your goods suffer, or the minute the delivery deadlines are missed, that's the moment when your business will be at its most vulnerable.

Therefore it is in your best interest to expend a fair amount of energy selecting who will manufacture your product or products.

VAs

Over the years our clients have said a good VA is invaluable in handling customer inquiries such as returns or negative reviews.

FINANCES

The starting point for effectively managing your finances is the preparation of a budget plan, product costing and a profit and loss statement.

Unless you have a full grasp of all – we repeat all – the costs associated with your business, you will be driving blind and as we all know that ultimately ends in a crash.

TAXES

There are two principle reasons to stay on top of your taxes: first, taxes represent a major portion of your product costings. Keeping them current and in good order will allow you to understand fully what your profit margins are. Secondly, any falling behind with taxes carries with it the possibility of your business being suspended, with the net result of your investment being lost.

ADVERTISING/MARKETING

While we consider all the component pieces of an e-commerce business to be important, it is the advertising and marketing elements that are at the heart of your business and will ultimately determine its success.

It should also be noted that advertising in the e-commerce realm is a discipline with many different parts, all of which have to fit neatly together in order to be effective. A logical jumping-off point to understand this world is to get a look at a Pay Per Click (PPC) strategy.

LOOK BEFORE YOU LAUNCH

Once you've established your business, with all the focus that requires, both on your product offering and the inherent administrative requirements, it is time to think about expanding outside your home borders.

The challenge to that expansion is picking the right marketplace(s) to sell in in order to reach the appropriate client base and be comfortable that both logistics and administration are in good hands.

We hope you've enjoyed this guide and found it useful. In the appendices, we have provided you with a checklist on how diversified your business is (Appendix I) and 12 tips for selling online (Appendix II). The e-commerce world is ever-expanding and if you have the commitment and energy to participate, it can be very rewarding.

APPENDIX I

☑ **1** Have you recently prepared a cashflow forecast/stress test for your business?

☐ **2** Have you studied your competitors and their online presence?

☐ **3** Are you familiar with your optimum price per SKU?

☐ **4** Are you confident with your existing sourcing and packaging services?

☐ **5** Are you able to calculate the frequency of replenishing your existing stock?

☐ **6** Have you diversified your e-commerce platforms?

☐ **7** Have you scaled your products horizontally and/or diagonally?

☐ **8** Have you got a plan B in place? e.g. How easy is it to switch manufacturers?

☐ **9** Have you explored other opportunities and diversified your income investments?

☐ **10** Are you prepared to scale up your e-commerce business or stay at peak?

APPENDIX II

What to consider when trading online

12 TIPS TO SUCCEED AT EXPANDING YOUR E-COMMERCE BUSINESS

Follow these steps to successfully expand your e-commerce business globally:

✓ **1** RESEARCH, RESEARCH, RESEARCH

☐ **7** Have a plan B in terms of sourcing and trading strategies (seasonal items, etc.)

☐ **2** Set your goals and decide what you want to achieve.

☐ **8** 'Cheap' doesn't mean that you will always generate a profit.

☐ **3** Find a balance between quality and quantity.

☐ **9** Remember that planning is the key to success.

☐ **4** Start with the largest marketplaces available to maximise sales potential.

☐ **10** Ensure that you have marketing and advertising streams in place.

☐ **5** Ensure that you stay compliant and engage an Accountant.

☐ **11** Don't abandon your basket (investigate as to why that may lead to abandonment of payment).

☐ **6** Localise your listings to ensure that your products are closer to your customers.

☐ **12** **Don't forget to pay yourself!**

111